THE DAY OF THE LORD

AN INTERPRETATION
OF THE BOOK OF REVELATION
AND OTHER
APOCALYPTIC SCRIPTURE
- WHAT IT IS: VOLUME II

Louis Diedricks

Two Harbors Press
212 3rd Avenue North, Suite 290
Minneapolis, MN 55401
612.455.2293
www.TwoHarborsPress.com

ISBN - 978-1-936198-05-4
ISBN - 1-936198-05-3
LCCN - 2009942759

Cover Design and Typeset by James Arneson

Printed in the United States of America

FORWARD AND WARNING

As many interpretations of the Bible's apocalypse abound, it then becomes obvious that many versions are wrong.

Without backing or reason supplied as to why many apocalyptic interpretations assess data as they do, this volume, The Day of the Lord, instead coordinates apocalyptic scriptures throughout the Old and New Testaments that describe the same set of circumstances, after which, when available, these data are then coordinated along with scientific conjecture and ongoing events. This in turn provides a more thorough understanding as to what is being described within apocalyptic text and what is said will come about when the Day of the Lord arrives.

Therefore, to all believers reading this page, be forewarned, for just as the contents within Pandora's jar could not again be sealed within, so too herein will many wish what is revealed had remained sealed. But as what it is swiftly nears, it is better to know than not what lies ahead for all mankind.

Woe to those who long for the day of the Lord! What good will the day of the Lord do you? It is darkness and not light—as when a man flees from a lion only to have a bear fall on him; then he runs into the house and leans his hand against the wall only to have a serpent bite him. Is not the day of the Lord darkness and not light, gloom with no gleam in it?

(Amos 5:18–20)

While recent scientific data indicates the earth may soon experience environmental catastrophes similar to those described for apocalyptic events in the Bible, beyond this preliminary corroboration for what lies in earth's future, science and theism part ways. The reason for this is science's dependence on physical evidence in order to make predictions, whereas biblical prophesy, not backed by physical evidence, is contingent upon faith in its relating God's word on future events.

However, given science's recent track record, where only five short years ago nearly all environmental models predicted a century and longer before most of the earth's ice masses would incur significant melting, with many of these same models now indicating an unexplained increase in ice melting, and with these models having adjusted their forecasts to meet the data as it arrived, their credibility in accurately predicting when or where climatic conditions will change in the future appears dubious at best.

And if the sciences have severe limitations in accurately predicting future events within their own realms of expertise, in regards to individuals' actions and policies for the future the sciences have virtually no capacity in predicting these types of outcomes—which then leaves the only other widely accepted means of seeing how these types of events will play out in the future: coming from faith in God and biblical scripture.

Because of such, the primary focus of this book deals with data provided throughout the Old and New Testaments of the Bible that relate to future events.

However, as many new scientific environmental models are now corroborating those of apocalyptic environmental conditions and also providing data pertaining to the cause for these calamities, scientific data and conjecture will therefore further assist in better understanding various apocalyptic scripture.

Folklore

Despite the vast quantities of apocalyptical text throughout the Bible that describe the same end-of-days events, each of these scriptures having multiple interpretations has had the effect of leaving most individuals, including theologians, in a quandary as to which, if any, interpretations are valid.

The primary cause for why so many conflicting interpretations exist is the vague imagery these scriptures produce through various factors. One of these factors is the style of writing these texts are often depicted in, which often results in leaving the vast majority of individuals clueless as to what they are relating, and because of such they have resulted in numerous interpretations.

One example of this style of writing was described in *What It Is, Volume 1* in regards to the creation; in order for Genesis 1:1 through Genesis 1:3 to be in accordance with scientific conjecture, these verses would have to be in *retrospect* of each other—Gen. 1:3 of Gen. 1:2, and Gen. 1:2 of Gen. 1:1.

The same holds true of the style of writing often associated with apocalyptic text, which when presented in a sequential format results in a convoluted perception and misinterpretation of the data.

Therefore, when viewing these scriptures in their proper format—retrospectively—much of what is currently perceived as gibberish in a sequential format will instead appear logically structured.

Another area causing ambiguity within apocalyptic text in conjunction with a sequential perspective is that these events are often described as if they have already occurred, when as of 2009 the majority of apocalyptic events have yet to commence.

One example of this, and probably the first description of an event relating to the end of days, is that of an individual only seven generations from Adam named Enoch, who according to Jude 1:14-15 quotes:

"Behold, the Lord has come with His myriads of holy ones to execute judgment against all, and to convict all the ungodly for all their impious activities which in their godlessness they have practiced, and for all the harsh words those godless sinners have spoken against Him."

Although Enoch spoke these words almost 6,000 years ago, as the acts contained therein have yet to transpire, this scripture is then in retrospect from a futuristic outlook and illustrates the retrospective manner of writing used in describing numerous apocalyptic events throughout the Bible.

A more elaborate example of this is illustrated by the apostle Paul in chapter four of the book of Hebrews when describing the seventh day on which God rests as a period set to occur physically in the future, after all events associated with the tribulation of the last days have concluded, thereby also indicating we are currently in the sixth day of creation (Diedricks 2008).

In conjunction with this retrospective style of writing, an extensive use of metaphors, describing everything from people, places, and events to spiritual entities and time, furthers the ambiguity of what is being conveyed by presenting images similar to that of a science fiction novel.

Adding to this ambiguity is what we today perceive as a catastrophic event, which pales by comparison to those describing apocalyptic events.

To put this in perspective, when we look at the December, 26, 2004 Indonesian tsunami that took over 230,000 lives, the Myanmar (formerly Burma) cyclone in May of 2008 that took 130,000 lives, and the earthquake in China shortly thereafter that took another 80,000 lives, many theologians perceived these catastrophes as evidence that events describing the apocalypse were upon us.

However, as these three catastrophes represent fewer than half a million lives (less than 0.01% of the earth's population), when placed in comparison with the number of individuals who will meet their demise during the days of tribulation, half a million lives correlates with less than an average day's mortality figure.

One example of this is provided in Isaiah chapter 24, describing the earth polluted to the point where intense heat severely affects agricultural production and the accompanying results are global depopulation (Diedricks 2008).

Being such, the loss of less than half a million lives, according to Mark 13:8 and Matthew 24:8, would constitute events preceding the days of apocalypse when earthquakes, wars, and other calamities will occur in various regions of the earth.

Although environmental catastrophes such as those depicted in the book of Isaiah chapter 24 confirm the worst of the apocalypse has yet to arrive, with many scientific environmental models now nearing par with Isaiah's environmental depictions for the not-too-distant future, the rest of Isaiah chapter 24's depiction of a depopulated planet appears more plausible.

By itself, however, Isaiah chapter 24 could be argued as representing any number of interpretations as well as time periods. But we will see when cross-referencing apocalyptic data from the book of Isaiah with other apocalyptic scripture from other books in the Bible that these will only fit together resulting in a single clear picture of events that are to transpire along with the days of apocalypse.

And as a few pieces of circumstantial evidence are often sufficient in determining the validity of something in a court of law, so too do numerous pieces of a puzzle that fit together producing a single clear picture provide greater credibility for these events on the whole, as they would otherwise be flawed with numerous inconsistencies detracting from their credibility.

Furthermore, as biblical apocalyptic scriptures were written over several centuries (thereby excluding collusion between scribes), to produce a concise and flaw-free clear depiction of events for the final period; although it is possible to have been a concerted work of fiction, where scribes over the centuries removed all possible flaws in order to deceive the general public, to have done so appears without motive.

Proceeding from the perspective that apocalyptic text is God's word, the next step will be choosing a primary point of reference in which to cross-reference other apocalyptic scripture throughout the other books in the Bible.

While various books from the Bible can be used for this purpose, the single source in the Bible containing the greatest amount of apocalyptic data is the book of Revelation in the New Testament. And because of other reasons, which shall shortly become clear, the book of Revelation will be the primary source in cross-referencing apocalyptic scripture in order to coordinate, corroborate, and clarify these events.

The Book of Revelation Elaborated

When reading through the book of Revelation, the first three chapters consist primarily of warnings to the seven churches of God throughout Asia Minor that, despite numerous temptations and tribulations, are exerted to maintain faith so that they may claim the prize (eternal life) as their reward.

After the warnings in the first three chapters, chapter 4 describes John being called to heaven, where he sees various entities.

In Revelation chapter 5 a scroll appears in heaven with seven seals that no one, either in heaven or on earth or under the earth, was able to open the scroll or to look inside it; at which point a sacrificed lamb (metaphor for the Lord Jesus Christ) appears and is found worthy to open the seven seals of the scroll.

After opening the first seal in Rev. 6:1, by Rev. 6:12 the sacrificed lamb (the Lord Jesus) has opened the sixth seal. Under these six seals the world experiences wars, lawlessness, famines, pestilence, earthquakes, genocide, and stars falling from heaven, as well as other calamities on earth and in heaven. This culminates with the kings of the earth, the nobles, the generals, the wealthy, the powerful, and others hiding themselves in the caves and in the mountain rocks from the presence of the One who is seated on the throne and from the wrath of the Lamb.

Despite that the seventh seal was not mentioned as having been opened within the verses in Revelation chapter 6, as the earth's inhabitants are at God's tribunal awaiting the dispensation of the Lords wrath, it would appear the seventh seal had to have been opened prior to this event.

But with the description of further calamities in chapter 7 proceeding those in chapter 6, and with the seventh seal still not mentioned opened in chapter 7, the predominant theorem among theologians continues to be that the end is not what is depicted with the closing statements in Revelation chapter 6.

However, when proceeding with Revelation, chapters 7–9, as many of the catastrophic events depicted appear identical with those in Revelation chapter 6 (wars, famines, pestilence, genocide, etc.), one of two possibilities then exists: either chapters 7–9 describe events following chapter 6 events with another round of the same type of calamitous events as those occurring in chapter 6, or chapters 7–9 are in retrospect of chapter 6.

But if in retrospect, one may then question, "Why was this additional material not simply placed in chapter 6?" Although the material in chapter 7 could have been incorporated into chapter 6, when reviewing chapter 6 in the book of Revelation we see that the main emphasis for this chapter appears in providing a synopsis as well as a sequential order for the events of the apocalypse, with latter chapters filling in with greater details the depictions portrayed in chapter 6.

One example of this is when reading Revelation 6:8–11 we see that the 25 percent of the world who have been killed during the fourth and fifth seals' events represents the Lord's people, of whom almost all of chapter 7 is dedicated upon elaborating in greater detail.

And while the seventh seal is still not mentioned opened in Revelation chapter 7; as Revelation 9:4 describes those who have God's seal issued to them in Rev. 7:3 not to be harmed by a certain species of locust, of whom the majority of these individuals are described deceased in Rev. 7:14–17; Rev. 9:4 then describes a period in Rev. 7:3–17 and Rev. 6:8–11 that is prior to these individuals' demise.

In which case, as Rev. 9:4 proceeds the seventh seal having being opened in Rev. 8:1, it would indicate that the seventh seal is open while events under the fourth and fifth seals are underway, thereby suggesting the seventh seal may also be open in conjunction with all other seals' events.

While this retrospective perspective of Revelation chapters 7–9 and chapter 6 with the seventh seal opened may be too controversial for some to accept, as we will soon see, there appear many instances throughout the Bible, including the book of Revelation, where the events being described precede those of the previous verse and/or chapter.

Another example of this is when nearing the end of Revelation chapter 14; here we are presented with a description of the earth's grapevine (metaphor for the earth's inhabitants) being harvested, thereby indicating no people on earth. But when Revelation chapter 15 commences, the earth appears miraculously repopulated. Therefore, in order for this data to be consistent with chapter 14, as well as with chapter 6, Revelation chapter 15 would have to be in retrospect to these previous chapters.

It is, however, easy to misconstrue a retrospective perspective for Revelation chapter 15 when in the first passage of Rev. 15:1 it states: "Then I saw another portent in heaven, great and marvelous—seven angels with seven plagues; *the last seven*, because with them God's wrath is completed."

When reading the phrase "the last seven," the initial impression the reader has is that these last seven plagues constitute an additional seven plagues to those in chapters 7–14, administered by seven different angels. However, when reading through chapters 15 and 16, as these seven plagues are being dispensed, we see these plagues appear strikingly similar in description to the seven plagues dispensed in Revelation chapters 7–14, as well as with the events described in Rev. chapter 6—thereby indicating these are the same plagues, but with yet more details provided. In which case, if these are the same plagues as those described in chapter 6, as well as those in chapters 7–14, the seventh seal would have been opened in Revelation chapter 6 despite not being mentioned until Revelation 8:1.

To corroborate the aforementioned conjecture we need to further assess whether the material for the book of Revelation is as described in retrospect of previous chapters, or if it is as many theologian societies currently believe it to be: in a sequential format without recapitulating on previous chapters.

To assume the latter option would suggest it could not be the word of God verbatim, as this produces incoherence and numerous inconsistencies. Whereas, assuming that much of the book of Revelation is written in retrospect, in addition to bringing structure and coherence to the data it would support the book of Revelation as God's word verbatim, transcribed by John as presented to him in an intentional format.

If, therefore, we further assume that the Lord has the capacity to have what He wants transcribed as He sees fit, the book of Revelation is then as the Lord intended. In which case this would also indicate that the book of Revelation was meant to become manifest at a specific time and not during John's time, as the data contained therein pertains primarily to events transpiring today.

Proceeding with the assumption that the book of Revelation is God's word verbatim depicting various apocalyptic data in a retrospective format that appear to be occurring today, the next step will be to correlate the data within the book of Revelation with itself and other apocalyptic scripture throughout the Bible in order to provide greater detail on how these events will come about.

To coordinate these events chronologically with each other and with current events, a linear timeframe reference is necessary. And as all apocalyptic events fall within the timeframes of the seven seals that are depicted in a complete chronological narrative from beginning to end in chapter 6 in the book of Revelation, chapter 6 will therefore represent the primary source for cross-referencing all apocalyptic text into a linear timeframe of events. This will provide a better perspective on what is being described and how they relate with events transpiring today and for the near future.

The First Seal

When the lamb—the Lord Jesus Christ—opens the first seal in Revelation 6:1-2, there appeared a white horse with a rider holding a bow; "...to him a crown was given, and he went out conquering and to conquer."

Many theories abound as to what this is in reference to, the least likely that this is in reference to an actual individual with a bow on a white horse going around conquering nations.

Therefore, realizing these as metaphors, the white horse and its rider are not a physical horse and rider as some suspect them to be, nor are they representative of supernatural beings as other theologian models suggest, but instead are metaphors representing a political affiliation and worldwide order during the days of the apocalypse.

The *crown* the first rider is given is a metaphor for *authority*, granted from heaven to undertake its task to conquer other nations. And the *bow* it utilizes to accomplish its conquests is a metaphor for *aerial* military action.

The fact that the rider of the white horse is under the first seal opened indicates this entity initiates apocalyptic events with his acts of conquering.

And with the world today approaching the final days; the white horse with its rider would represent a political affiliation of nations whose actions fit the description for conquering via aerial military assault.

Being such, and as motivation is necessary for any expensive military campaign of conquering others to occur, to do so usually represents the prospect of greater returns than the costs involved in such undertakings.

Therefore, with the rider of the white horse's method of conquering others profiled as aerial attacks and with a motivation of attaining greater returns than the costs involved with expensive military campaigns, the only recent candidate meeting this profile would have been the invasion of Iraq in 2003—with a sea of oil under its sands.

And if the invasion of Iraq in 2003 represents the commencement point for the first rider's conquests, the rider of the white horse would correspond with the US military while the white horse would represent the world's primary free-market nations, which also partook in Iraq's conquest and occupation.

However, as the reference in Revelation 6:1–2 suggests various conquests, it would indicate that, even when adding Afghanistan as a second conquest, these two conquests would only represent the first of a series of conquests that will be undertaken by the rider of the white horse.

At this point it appears we may need to wait for further developments to occur to see what other nations will come under the list of conquests by the rider of the white horse. But as mentioned previously, other books in the Bible provide additional data on the final period, one of which is the book of Daniel where Daniel 8:5-7 refers to a he-goat with a prominent horn that advances from the west over the whole earth without touching the ground, then attacks and defeats a ram with two horns, breaking both its horns. As the two horns the he-goat breaks are a metaphor for two military powers described in Daniel 8:20, and as the lands of Media and Persia that today correspond to the lands of Iran and Iraq, it then indicates the land of Iran will join Iraq in falling to the he-goat.

The next issue arises with Daniel 8:21 describing the he-goat that attacks Media and Persia (Iran and Iraq) as the king of Greece. But as the land of Greece does not fit the profile of the he-goat with the prominent horn traversing the whole earth without touching the ground, representing the world's prominent air force power traversing the whole earth in order to attack the two nations of Media and Persia (Iran and Iraq) during the days of apocalypse, we then realize Greece is a metaphor for a land from a futuristic perspective, exemplifying an equivalent status as Greece would have had in the sixth century BC during Daniel's days.

Therefore, when coordinating the invasion of Iraq in 2003 with the world's prominent air force responsible for its conquest, the US best fits the metaphoric profiles of the he-goat as well as the king of Greece.

Although the conquest of Iran has yet to be realized in 2009, as various conquests are inferred to the rider of the white horse in Rev. 6:1–2, and Daniel 8:5–7 describes Iraq as well as Iran falling to the he-goat, it would appear simply a matter of time before Iran's conquest occurs.

The Second Seal

When the lamb opened the second seal, a fiery red horse emerged whose "rider was empowered to take peace from the earth, so that people would kill one another, and a huge sword was given him" (Rev. 6:3–4).

The red horse, like the white horse, represents a political affiliation on the earth at the time of the apocalypse. And the huge sword it was provided is a metaphor for a vast arsenal of military capacity.

The fact that the rider of the red horse is empowered to take peace from the earth indicates this empowerment is authorized by God, while the people who will kill one another represent the various factions and nations under the second riders' authority who will self-annihilate in civil wars. And that this will be accomplished by means of a huge sword represents the vast military arsenal the rider of the red horse possesses.

Assuming these accurate assessments, this data would indicate that the skirmishes seen so far between Russia and various former Soviet republics, such as Azerbaijan and Soviet Georgia, will continue to escalate as this federation's socioeconomic system worsens, at which time several other former Soviet republics will also experience internal strife that will lead to civil unrest.

Another item to note here is that while actions are taken by the first rider of the white horse, the rider of the second horse would also in all likelihood be conducting affairs of state, thereby indicating an overlapping of events under the first and second seals.

The Third Seal

During and after events under the first two seals, when the lamb opens the third seal in Rev. 6:5–6 there emerges a black horse with a rider holding a pair of scales, at which time a being in heaven exclaims: "A quart of wheat for a day's wage and three quarts of barley for a day's wage, and do not damage the oil and the wine."

If we remain consistent with the former hypotheses for the first and second riders along with their horses representing groups of peoples and their socioeconomic systems (white for capitalism, red for communism), the rider of the black horse would describe a third affiliation, hypothetically representing emerging nations previously referred to as Third World nations.

And as the description of food in exchange for labor indicates the world's economies will be in a state of disarray, this description is somewhat comparative to the period following the fall of the Roman Empire in the fifth century A.D. where, for nearly a millennium, Europe entered a period known as the Dark Ages (Diedricks 2008).

The color black in describing the third horse is actually a lack of color; this lack of color may represent a world in which global socio-economic inaction has taken place due to a lack of viable working alternatives.

The Fourth Seal

While events under the third seal's timeframe are going on (while little economically is going on) an alternative fourth system and its rider emerge.

When the fourth seal is opened in Rev. 6:7–8 we read: "...then I looked and saw an ash-colored horse. The name of its rider was Death, and Hades followed him closely. Authority was granted them over a quarter of the earth to kill with the sword, with famine, with plague, and by means of the wild beasts of the earth."

In comparison to the first three socioeconomic systems described, we are presented here with a description of what appear to be spiritual entities.

Although Death is described as the rider of the fourth ash-colored horse, if this rider were, as the previous three riders, representing nations and administering a type of working socioeconomic system on the earth, it then appears genocide constitutes part of the fourth rider's working system.

With the fourth seal being opened representing a period in time after the third seal's work for sustenance program has been running for a while, it would appear to indicate some sort of environmental catastrophe has occurred initiating famine conditions throughout the globe, and thereby ushering in the fourth rider's reign, who will then initiate a global genocide against 25 percent of the worlds population.

If this were to occur today, with an approximate global population of 6.5 billion people, it would represent 6.5 billion/4, or one billion six hundred and twenty five million people (1,625,000,000), who are to be killed under the fourth seal's timeframe.

And as a worldwide policy condoning genocide, where the difference between right and wrong are willfully ignored, the pale color description of the fourth horse (neither black, nor white, but shades of grey) may be seen as describing an amoral attitude at this time.

Although it may seem implausible to many that the spiritual entity Death will, through some individual and/or world power, initiate a fourth worldwide socioeconomic system where 25 percent of the world's populace will be killed through various means of genocide, if we look at how individuals and nations have historically reacted when resources did not suffice for the masses we see that many reactions have often been similar to those initiated by Nazi Germany during world war II—or as is currently the case in the Darfur region of Sudan, Africa today.

Therefore, if the first method described in Rev. 6:8 for the elimination of 25 percent of the world's populace is the sword, it would represent hundreds of millions of individuals that will perish through direct executions.

The second description for the elimination of 25 percent of the world's populace by means of famine would also represent hundreds of millions of individuals, who will perish through deprivation of access to sustenance.

The third description for the elimination of 25 percent of the world's populace via pestilence is a combination of weakened immune systems due to a lack of proper nourishment in conjunction with plague conditions that will emerge with millions of unburied bodies from the first two means of genocide.

In support of this conjecture, historical records show time and again that, after many major military campaigns have left large quantities of corpses, the rotting corpses soon created plague conditions that quickly spread to neighboring regions (Diedricks 2008).

Wild Beasts

The fourth and probably most controversial means of genocide mentioned in Revelation 6:8 is by the wild beasts of the earth.

The reason for this is that, given the number of predatory beasts in the world that account for as many as several thousand mortalities annually today, if the fourth means of death described in Rev. 6:8 represents millions of individuals, it appears improbable that the wild beasts of the earth could account for anything more than several tens of thousands of mortalities under the fourth and fifth seals' timeframes.

This may be explained by one of two different possibilities.

Given that the fourth means of death in Revelation 6:8 is the last and hypothetically least of the four causes for deaths under the fourth and fifth seals' timeframes, the number of individuals who will die by these means may represent only several tens of thousands of individuals, in which case the current number of deaths annually by wild beasts would suffice.

The second possibility is that death by wild beasts will account for millions of individuals over the course of the fourth and fifth seals' timeframes. As implausible as this currently sounds, there is new environmental data indicating this scenario is more plausible than only a few short years ago.

The reason for this is that one of the side effects of higher CO_2 levels producing warmer temperatures on the earth has been an increase in the size and numbers of various animal and plant species, with some species of bees having acquired more aggressive characteristics. In Alaska, severe stings from bees, wasps, and yellow jackets in some areas have increased by as much as 600 percent in eight years (Tolme 2008).

Although this is currently a far cry from being able to kill millions of individuals, as global warming intensifies and mutational characteristics among species intensify, it is then just a matter of time before one or more mutations among insect species will have extremely dire effects on other animal species, including humans.

The Devonian and Carboniferous Periods

In further support of this perspective, over the last 500 million years there have only been a handful of times CO_2 levels in the earth's atmosphere have reached levels as high as today.

A couple of these periods when levels of CO_2 in the atmosphere were as high or higher than those of today were the Devonian and Carboniferous periods, which occurred approximately 400 million to 300 million years ago.

At the onset of the Devonian period (approximately 400 million years ago), few animal and plant species existed on dry land. But over several tens of millions of years, as CO_2 levels in the atmosphere rose significantly, carbon sequestration (the removal of carbon from the atmosphere) commenced with the appearance of many new animal and plant species. Because of this the Devonian period came to a close and the Carboniferous period began.

As a proliferation of species emerged throughout the Carboniferous, many insects arose that appeared similar to today's insects, except that by comparison they were significantly larger than their modern-day counterparts; there were dragonflies with wingspans nearly three feet across, cockroaches about one foot in length, and six-foot-long centipedes. ("Monsters of the Past")

While some paleontologists attribute the cause for gigantism during the Carboniferous to greater levels of oxygen in the atmosphere than the 21 percent of O_2 in the atmosphere seen today, carbon sequestration was a primary component in the proliferation of species that would also have played an integral role in the gigantism among insect type species.

Therefore, while CO_2 levels in our atmosphere today may not be as high as levels during the Devonian and Carboniferous periods, making it unlikely insects will mutate to such enormous proportions as those seen then, this data does nonetheless lend support that, as levels of CO_2 in the atmosphere continue to rise, further mutational characteristics will produce larger and fiercer species of insects, some of which will carry new pathogens that will account for the demise of many individuals in the near future.

The Fifth Seal

When the fifth seal is opened in Rev. 6:9–11, it commences with a description of "the souls of those who had been slaughtered for the sake of the word of God and the witness they bore."

Since the fifth seal follows the events for the preceding seal, where 25 percent of mankind is killed, the fifth seal in Rev. 6:9–11 is then describing the aftermath of those who have met their demise during the fourth seal's timeframe. This also indicates the actions under the fourth seal will overflow into the fifth seal's timeframe, thereby supporting that actions within the seven seals' timeframes do overlap each other's timeframes to varying degrees.

The Sixth Seal

Following the fifth seal, when the sixth seal is opened in Rev. 6:12–17, various descriptions of apocalyptic events are presented that culminate with the earth's remaining inhabitants hiding themselves from the presence of the One seated in heaven.

One item differentiating the sixth seal from the previous five seals is that events are now also occurring in the heavens, whereas the first five seals events were primarily focused on the earth.

Of the celestial items under the sixth seal, the stars of heaven are described falling to the earth. Realizing the fall of the stars as yet another metaphor, we then refer to other biblical scripture to see what these stars falling from heaven to earth represent.

Hebrews 12:26 states: "Once more I will shake, not only the earth, but heaven as well." This shaking of heaven and earth is further elaborated in the following verse of Hebrews 12:27, referring to "...the removal of everything shaken-created things, so that the unshaken things remain."

As the entire universe and its contents, however, have been created by God, the reference to created things is not to those created by God, but to those self-created apart from the Lord, which are corrupt and when put to the test, will shake until ultimately collapsing.

Therefore, with the shaken/created things representing those apart from God to be shaken out; when Revelation 12:9 describes the great dragon, the serpent of old, called the devil and Satan, along with his angels being forced out from heaven and flung to the earth; the devil with his angels would then represent those that are to be shaken out from heaven.

And with Revelation 6:13 describing the stars from heaven falling to the earth, this metaphoric description would appear to describe the devil and his angels, in which case it would also illustrate a retrospective description of Rev. 6:13 with Rev. 12:9.

I would like to point out another statement from Luke 10:18, where the Lord Jesus is quoted saying, "... I saw Satan fall from heaven like lightning."

Although Satan falling from heaven like lightning was described some two thousand years ago; as the devil and his angels have yet to be expelled from heaven in 2009, this statement then constitutes one made in retrospect to a future event that will constitute the shakeout from heaven described in Hebrews 12:26–27, and in Rev. 6:13 and Rev. 12:9.

After Satan and his angels will have been forced out of heaven and cast to the earth, Rev. 12:12 then states: "...Woe to the earth and the sea, because the devil has come down to you with raging anger, well aware that he has but a short season."

This data, where woe is described occurring to both earth and sea due to the devil's raging anger for having been cast to the earth, when placed in conjunction with Revelation 13:1–2 where the dragon-Satan invests his power and his throne and great authority to the beast with 10 horns and seven heads that emerges from the sea; it indicates the dragon will achieve his malicious intents to both earth and sea through the beast. This will be further elaborated upon in a later chapter.

After Revelation Chapter Six

After replacing various metaphors for the first three riders with identities associating them with current events, we see that many of the depictions for the first three riders' actions do not occur sequentially, but instead transpire concurrently, indicating events under each of the first three seals' timeframes do not conclude before events under the next seals' timeframes commence, further suggesting events under seals four through seven will likewise interact with other seals' timeframes to varying degrees.

Furthermore, as events between different entities occurring concurrently appear more plausible than one where a series of events under one seal concludes before events under the next seal commence, the timeframes associated with apocalyptic events appear more reasonable.

However, despite more plausibility with various seals' events running concurrently than consecutively with each other, the time spans often depicted with all entities and events in association with the days of tribulation appear to conflict with aforementioned assessments as to who various of these entities and events represent.

To clarify: having previously assessed the rider of the white horse conquering Iraq and Afghanistan in 2003 as representing the initiation of apocalyptic events, and given that the two most widely used timeframes associated with the days of tribulation constitute a 1,290-day (3.5-year; 42-month) or a 2,300-day time period, an April 2003 commencement for the rider of the white horse's conquering of nations, even if representing the onset of events within the 2,300-day period, those days would have expired by the end of 2009.

In this case, to answer this discrepancy we need to look at the data in relation to the timeframes described.

When the days of tribulation are described, they are usually in association with the reign of an entity known as the antichrist, who will represent the worst of times man has ever seen (Matthew 24:15–22; Mark 13:14–20).

Being such, and as these timeframes are specifically in association with the antichrist, although the first three riders and their actions constitute the first three seals within the book of Revelation, their actions do not per se constitute either the 1,290-day (3.5-year; 42-month) period or the 2,300-day period in association with the antichrist's reign.

In which case, the next item would be ascertaining when the time periods in association with the antichrist are to commence.

Although Revelation chapter 6 provides a complete chronological synopsis of the apocalypse, we see that the antichrist is not directly mentioned within the seven seals. Nonetheless, realizing the seven seals encompass the entire apocalypse, it then stands to reason that the antichrist is present and active within the narrative of the seals described. This being the case, locating where within the seven seals the antichrist is active will then point to when the worst of apocalyptic events constituting the 1,290-day and the 2,300-day periods are to occur, and this will also provide reference in relation to the other seals' timeframes and events.

Before proceeding in locating the antichrist within the seven seals timeframes, in order to retrieve all possible data on this individual, a definition of the word "antichrist" is necessary.

One item to realize is that the word "antichrist" appears only five times in the first and second epistles of John, and being such, it appears somewhat odd that so much emphasis has been placed on this individual. The reason so much emphasis has been placed on this individual is that although only five scriptures use the term "antichrist" in reference to an individual who will undertake various negative actions during the days of the tribulation, throughout the Bible there also appear various metaphors used in association with an individual who during the days of tribulation will undertake numerous negative actions such as those described in association with the antichrist, and because of such have been deemed by many theologian societies to represent the same individual. These other descriptions of the antichrist will appear and be elaborated upon when related topics raise his profile in forthcoming chapters.

Another item that will need to be addressed is that although there is one primary antichrist there have been, are, and will be many antichrists, as this also is mentioned in the epistles of John.

As 1 John 2:22 says, "Who is the liar if it is not the one who denies that Jesus is the Christ? He is the antichrist who denies the Father and the Son."

By definition, the answer provided to this question is synonymous with atheism, and therefore 1 John constitutes atheists as antichrists.

And as 1 John 2:22 defines "antichrist" as an atheist, with 1 John 2:18 describing many antichrists, he is then describing many who are atheist.

But while these descriptions relate to many antichrists, 1 John 2:18 also refers to an antichrist (in the singular) who is to make his appearance during the final days of tribulation. When cross-referencing this entity's various depictions throughout the Bible, the combined data will further our understanding on how this individual will interact with world affairs that will bring about the worst of times for mankind.

666-616

Probably the best known description in association with the antichrist is the number of the beast—666—described in Rev. 13:18. However, as no data in association with either the name or number of the beast exists, we then need to refer to the antichrist's profile in order to locate correlating data that will provide a better understanding as to what the second beast's name and number represent.

Revelation 13:16–17 describes the mark of the beast as a name or a number that will be issued to everyone on either their hand or forehead in order to conduct any and all sorts of transactions.

Those who will refuse to accept his name or number on their hand or forehead are to be killed under a global policy of genocide initiated by the antichrist. And as these individuals represent the global Christian community who will refuse the mark of the beast, they also then represent the 25 percent of the world's inhabitants terminated under the fourth and fifth seals' timeframes described in Rev. 6:8–11, as well as in Rev. chapter 7.

And as these events are accredited to the rider of the fourth ash-colored horse, though he is described as Death in Rev. 6:8, he also represents the antichrist.

In which case, as the antichrist is the one who will initiate the mark of the beast that will be responsible for the demise of those who will not accept the beast's mark, and as this represents the tribulation period of the Lord's people that constitutes 1,290 days (Rev. 13:5–7), the fourth and fifth seals' timeframes then represent this time period.

As to when the antichrist will initiate this action, with Daniel 9:27 describing a one-week period (seven years) in which the antichrist will cause the covenant (new world order) to prevail with many and that in the middle of the week he will cause sacrifice and offering to cease, it indicates that halfway through the antichrist's seven-year period of influence in world affairs will be the point on which the 1,290-day tribulation period of the Lord's people will commence.

This event is also described in Mark 13:14 and Matthew 24:15–16, where those in Judea, when they see the desolating abomination set up in the holy place, should then flee to the mountains; 2 Thessalonians 2:3–4 describes this holy place as the temple in Jerusalem, where the antichrist will stand and declare himself as God.

Therefore, as the antichrist is scheduled to initiate a globally sanctioned genocide against the world's predominant religion—Christianity—and as this scenario appears impossible today, we then need to see what scriptures say will transpire that will cause the world to accept and even authorize the antichrist to commence genocidal policies.

In Daniel 7:1–7, four beasts are described metaphorically, representing the four leading socioeconomic systems during the days of apocalypse. Daniel 7:7 describes the fourth beast as having 10 horns and devouring and tearing its victims to pieces while stamping the remains with its feet. This fourth beast with 10 horns is also mentioned in Revelation 13:1–3 as having seven heads, one of which is fatally wounded and then resuscitated.

Having previously established that the four horsemen of the apocalypse in chapter 6 of Revelation also represent the world's four leading socioeconomic systems at the time of the apocalypse, these entities would then be the same, though they are described metaphorically different.

Therefore, by coordinating the description of the fourth beast with those of the four horsemen of the apocalypse, we see that the profile for the rider of the white horse in Revelation 6:1–2 who goes about conquering others best applies with the description for the fourth beast with iron teeth that goes about tearing its victims to pieces, while stamping the remains with its feet.

The reason why the second horseman of the apocalypse does not fit this profile is because he is not directly credited with disposing of his adversaries but instead has them killing each other.

And while the fourth horseman of the apocalypse could fit this profile, as he is accredited with killing many, with forthcoming details that will appear as this volume proceeds we will see this being is not the beast with seven heads and 10 horns.

In which case, if the fourth beast with seven heads and 10 horns and the rider of the white horse is the same primary socioeconomic power during the end of days, the seven heads would represent the primary free-market nations, of which the G-7, represented by seven nations, the US, Canada, Britain, France, Italy, Germany, and Japan constitute its economic heads.

In which case, the fatally wounded head described in Rev. 13:3 would indicate an economic malaise with one of its heads, which severely affects the other heads of the G-7.

While this economic malaise is transpiring, Revelation 13:4 then describes the fatally wounded head of the beast resuscitated and the world *worshiping* the dragon and the beast as a result.

As we now realize, the fatally wounded head of the beast does not represent a supernatural entity; this scripture connoting other surreal depictions is anything but what it appears superficially.

In regards to the word "worship," although the definition can include the performance of religious services and exercises, a more correct definition is a deeply felt adoration that may or not include outwardly expression.

In which case, as true worship is synonymous with adoration, and with the Bible describing an honest adoration by the majority of the earth's inhabitants towards the dragon and the beast, this adoration will result in conjunction with the resuscitation of the fatally wounded head.

Some may now reason, even if the world were to come out of an economic depression with the resuscitation of the beast's fatally wounded head, they would not necessarily worship the dragon and the beast as a result.

The primary reason for this premise is the sci-fi imagery worshiping the dragon and the beast currently presents.

By correlating data, however, from other biblical scripture in what the dragon stands for, these will then produce a more realistic depiction that will explain why the majority of mankind will voluntarily worship the dragon.

As the devil is master over those living for their flesh (Galatians 5:17; Galatians 6:8; Ephesians 4:19; 2 Peter 2:19), when in Revelation 13:4 the dragon bestows authority to the beast whose fatally wounded head was completely resuscitated in Revelation 13:3, it indicates that the beast's socioeconomic policies will morph into one that will further spread a worldwide lifestyle based on hedonistic values.

This perspective is corroborated when comparing the book of Daniel and the book of Revelation's descriptions of the world's nations during the end times.

Daniel 7:3–9 describes four large animals that rise from the sea (leopard, bear, lion, and a beast with 10 horns and iron teeth); these animals in Daniel 7:17 are described independent to each other and represent the four kingdoms that shall arise out of the earth prior to when the saints of the Most High shall receive the kingdom (thereby indicating the end times).

In comparison, when Revelation 13:1–2 describes the fourth beast, although it has the same 10 horns, this beast now has seven heads and seven diadems. More importantly, it has the features of the first three animals (leopard, bear, and lion), which were described independent of each other in Daniel 7:3–8, thereby indicating all the world's nations will be joined in a unified endeavor under the fourth beast when the dragon bestows authority on it and heals the mortally wounded head. (Rev. 13:3–4)

Therefore, as the world worshiping the dragon and the beast after resuscitation from an economic depression in association with the fatally wounded head indicates the world's enamored status with the hedonistic lifestyle the dragon and the beast will provide; this endeavor is elaborated in Revelation 18:3: "For all the nations have drunk the wine of her passionate immorality, and the kings of the earth have committed fornication with her, and the merchants of the earth have grown rich on her abundance of wantonness."

As to who Rev. 18:3 is in reference to, Rev. 18:2 describes her as "Babylon the Great," and she is described two verses earlier in Rev. 17:18 as "the great city that has dominion over the kings of the earth."

And by having dominion over the kings of the earth, the implication is that Babylon the Great will impose its economic policies on the world's nations propagating its hedonistic values worldwide that will result in the consequences described in Rev. 18:3.

Being chief economic policymaker for the world would also suggest that Babylon the Great represents the primary head of the beast that is to be resuscitated from the fatal wound. The reason for this is if one of the lesser heads were the one fatally wounded, it would represent less of a threat to the viability of the beast's system than its primary head would.

Another issue this raises, however, is that if the beast's seven heads represent the G-7 nations, how can any city represent one of its seven heads?

The most probable answer for this may be that, just as imperial Rome during antiquity was only a city but also represented parts of Europe, Asia, and Africa, so too is the status between Babylon the Great and the beast's other members—the G-7 today.

Also contesting the possibility of Babylon the Great representing one of the beast's seven heads is that Rev. 17:3 describes Babylon as "a woman seated upon a scarlet beast covered with blasphemous titles. It had seven heads and 10 horns."

When reading this verse, the immediate impression is that the beast being described is the one with seven heads and 10 horns, and the woman is a separate entity. But, as the latter part of Rev. 17:3 states: "It had seven heads and 10 horns," and as the woman (Babylon the Great) is included within this description, she is then one of the beast's members.

And as the portrayal of the woman depicted in Rev. 17:3–5 is one where she enjoys a free ride on the back of the beast, it further supports Babylon as the beast's primary head. In which case, with "Babylon the Great" representing the head economic policymaker of the world's nations that includes the G-7, the city that best fits this description and of having dominion over the kings of the earth today is New York City.

But as a result of having to support the woman, Rev 17:16-17 states: "The 10 horns and the beast will hate the harlot and make her desolate and naked; they will consume her flesh and burn her up with fire. For God has put into their hearts to work His purpose, and to act harmoniously in handing their kingdom to the beast until the words of God should be fulfilled."

As the beast is described harmoniously handing their kingdom to the beast; the receiving beast represents the antichrist to whom the primary beast's members will hand over their kingdom (Babylon) to be obliterated through the various means described in Rev. 17:16.

The Cause of Babylon the Great's Demise

While much of the world today loathes NYC's financial sector for having created the global recession through the manipulation of various financial instruments that caused credit worldwide to come to a halt, according to the book of Daniel these appear to be merely coincidentally running events behind what will further precipitate the beasts other members to obliterate Babylon. To see why this is, we first need to recapitulate on various events which have transpired over the last several years that have helped bring about today's global economic climate.

As everything that is produced, transported, distributed, and maintained requires energy that in the US, in large part, is imported from the Middle East in the form of crude oil. With the initial motivating factor for conquering Iraq in 2003 being for its oil reserves, of which the rider of the white horse (the he-goat with the prominent horn) representing the US and its military have had the role of primary participant, military expenditures associated with this role have added anywhere from just under one trillion dollars to several trillion dollars, depending upon ones source of data, to the US's deficit over the last eight years.

In addition, when Daniel 8:8 describes the prominent horn of the he-goat being broken after having broken both horns of Media and Persia—Iraq and Iran—and assuming gigantic proportions, the gigantic proportions that cause the he-goat's horn to be broken are the immense costs associated with the enlarged status of the US' borders, which as of 2009 have yet to incorporate campaign expenses that will be associated in conquering Iran.

Being such, as these campaigns outside of the 50 contiguous United States are financed through foreign entities who expect a decent rate of return from a stable currency; with the US in the future projected to have to print trillions of additional dollars to compensate for its gigantic proportions overseas, the dollar will then become a less secure financial instrument, and as a result many of the US's financiers will withdraw from purchasing US securities, which will then further prompt the US Treasury to print even more currency to finance its expansion overseas, ultimately resulting in a drastically devalued US dollar.

Therefore, while the current global economic recession is due to the US's manipulation of the real estate market and its credit markets coming to a halt, the depiction of the fatally wounded head describing an economic depression appears will be due to the US's military in maintaining their gigantic proportions overseas.

Another item requiring explaining is how and why the price for a barrel of oil dropped so dramatically in the latter half of 2008, which in turn helped stabilize the world's economies throughout 2009.

The official spiel here has been that the drop in price for oil reflects decreased demand for oil as the world entered the ongoing global recession.

While it is true that demand for oil and its derivatives dropped as a result of the global recession, this drop in demand represents approximately a 10 percent drop from 2008 levels and therefore would not account for a near 50 percent drop in price from its 2008 peak.

Another reason used in explaining what caused oil's precipitous drop in price in 2008 was the manipulation of this commodity's futures market. The problem with this explanation, however, is that OPEC nations would voluntarily had to have been willing to accept a 50 percent decrease in their GDPs (gross domestic product earnings).

As the aforementioned criteria therefore do not provide credibility in explaining oil's dramatic plunge in price that commenced in July of 2008, we then need to look at other events transpiring at the time that would have played a significant role in the rapid decline in fuel prices.

In July of 2008, as the price for a barrel of oil hit a new high ($147 a barrel), the nation of Libya, which had for decades been regarded as a renegade nation under Colonel Muammar Ghadaffi's guidance, had for some time been in negotiations with western nations to make amends for prior wrongs. After regaining recognition status with various G-7 nations throughout 2006 and 2007, in July 2008 the United States officially recognized Libya as a member nation and reinstated it with full diplomatic status.

This reinstatement into the fold of nations was officially recognized as being due to Libya's Colonel Muammar Ghadaffi giving billions of dollars in restitution to the nations and individuals on which numerous acts of terrorism had been carried out over the several decades of his tenure.

Once reinstated with full diplomatic status, Colonel Ghadaffi immediately opened Libya's oil fields to western nations, at which time—coincidently—the price of oil commenced its downward spiral.

While not officially the reason for oil's dramatic drop in price, had it not been for Libya's opening of its oil fields to the G-7 nations at this time, the global economic recession from the latter half of 2008 and throughout 2009 would have been worse and may have even precipitated an economic collapse on a global scale.

In which case, if Ghadaffi making Libya's oil reserves available to the G-7 nations helped in bringing down the price of oil, thereby stabilizing the global economy, it would show he played an integral role in resuscitating the beast's economic malaise at this time.

If we then coordinate this data with Daniel 11:43, where in describing the antichrist Daniel quotes: "The Libyans and the Ethiopians shall be in his retinue," as the definition of the word "retinue" in this instance describes servants, with Colonel Ghadaffi having had the Libyan people in his retinue for over the last three decades, he then fits the first half of this profile.

Furthermore, with Revelation 13:14 describing a second beast who comes up from the land having two horns like a lamb; as the antichrist will have the Ethiopians as well as the Libyans in his retinue, and the two lambs' horns connote two nations with nominal military capacity, this lends further support to the two horns described in Daniel 11:43 representing Libya and Ethiopia, thereby establishing second beast as the antichrist.

Corroborating the profile in Rev. 13:14, where the antichrist's initial military capacity will be nominal, Daniel 8:34 states: "His power shall be mighty, but not by force of arms; in astonishing ways he shall bring ruin..."

In which case with the antichrist bringing ruin to others via non-militaristic means; when Daniel 7:8 describes a little horn (another metaphor for the antichrist) through which three of the beasts 10 horns are uprooted (defeated), the depiction of a little horn describes the antichrist's military capacity at the time when he uproots three of the beasts' 10 horns, as nominal.

However, as these references to the antichrists military capacity as nominal are in reference to when he emerges, when Daniel 8:9 describes the little horn growing very large after commencing small, it indicates the antichrists military power will eventually grow.

This is further corroborated when Daniel 11:38 states: "…he shall honor the god of fortresses; with gold and silver, with precious stones and jewelry he will honor a god whom his fathers never knew," indicating the antichrist will use much of the wealth he attains during his reign within the system of the beast to purchase military installations.

Despite that Colonel Ghadaffi is currently the best candidate meeting most of the criteria associated with the antichrist, there remains one issue that appears to disqualify him. With the definition of the word "antichrist" synonymous with "atheism," and with Colonel Ghadaffi declaring faith in Allah, the title of antichrist would appear not to describe him.

However, as it is common practice for many politicians to declare faith in God and/or Allah in order to curry favor with their constituents; with Matthew 7:16–20 stating: "You will know them by the deeds they do," those politicians whose actions contradict behavior associated with faith in God are then in all likelihood merely paying lip service in order to maintain their political status, while in reality they are void of faith in God and/or Allah.

But as the true nature of many individuals' faith remains ambiguous, we then need more data in relation with the antichrist to further substantiate who he represents.

Probably the most widely known bit of data on the antichrist is the number 666, described in Revelation 13:18.

The first item requiring explaining with this scripture, however, is that the long-held idea that the number 666 represents the number of the beast has recently been proven to be an ancient typo.

"In May 2005, it was reported that scholars at Oxford University using advanced imaging techniques had been able to read illegible portions of the earliest known record of the Book of Revelation, from the Oxyrhynchus site, Papyrus 115 or p115, dating to the mid to late third century. The fragment gives the Number of the Beast as 616 (chi, iota, stigma), rather than the majority text 666 (chi, xi, stigma). The other early witness Codex Ephraemi Rescriptus (C) has it written in full: hexakosisi deka hex (lit. six hundred sixteen)." ("Number of the Beast" 2009)

Being such, when referencing Revelation 13:18: "Here intelligence comes in. Let him who has the mind for it calculate the number of the beast, for it is a man's number, and his number is 666," and realizing 666 as an ancient typo that actually represents 616, the next step is to assess how the number 616 is in reference to a man's number.

But before proceeding with this assessment, we first need to ask, to which beast is the number 616 in reference to? Is it in reference to the antichrist (which is currently the most popularly held consensus by theologians), or is it in reference to the primary beast with 10 horns and seven heads?

As Revelation 13:18 clearly specifies it as being the number of a man, the consensus has been that it represents the antichrist.

However, although it will relate directly with a man (the antichrist) as the antichrist-the little horn—will become one with the primary beast, as specified in Daniel 7:8, it then also designates the number 616 in association with the primary beast's socioeconomic system, which will include its other members.

Being such, the next step will be in assessing how the number 616 references a man (the antichrist) and his association with the primary beast.

Previous speculations for what 666 meant included counting the number of letters in an individual's name, such as Ronald Wilson Reagan, which led some to speculate Reagan represented the antichrist. But with 616 representing the number of the antichrist, this hypothesis would require utilizing only Reagan's middle initial in order for this method to work and would still not provide a feasible explanation as to how this number would represent an individual, as numerous individuals would fit this criterion.

Therefore, as this hypothesis lacks viability, a more feasible approach would be to first acquire a definition of the word "number" from which reasonable assessments can then be made.

One of the original definitions of "number" is *whence*, describing *from when* in relation to time. And when a number is used to reference an individual or an event in relation to time, it is often in association with a commencement or termination point, an example of this being the old cliché "his number is up" referring to an individual's time to die, thereby referencing a chronological point in time.

Assuming then that time is a feasible assessment in referencing a man's number, the next step is to assess what chronological point in time 616 may refer to. By further assuming the birth of Jesus Christ is the point of embarkation, and by knowing that Jesus was born between 4 and 8 BC ("Birth of Christ" 2009); 616 would then represent the sixth month in one of four years from 2008 through 2012; that may or may not represent the month of June, as this assumes consistency with today's Gregorian calendar.

Therefore, seeing as full diplomatic relations between Ghadaffi, Libya, the US, and the world's other G-7 nations were fully restored in July 2008 and this date correlates with the "whence" of 616, 616 could then commemorate this event as the commensuration point between the antichrist and the beast.

While this date also represents when Colonel Ghadaffi opened Libya's oil reserves to the system of the beast that helped bring down the price of oil from $140 a barrel in July 2008 to $40 by December 2008; having aided in averting a global economic meltdown, it appears that either in gratitude or in payment on February 2, 2009 "Moammar Ghadaffi of Libya was elected as leader of the African Union, a position long sought by the eccentric dictator..." (*Westchester Lower Hudson Journal News*, February 3, 2009)

Some may now question: what does Ghadaffi providing oil to

the west have to do with influencing African nations in electing him leader of the African Union? To answer this, a little history on Colonel Ghadaffi is necessary.

For more than thirty years, Colonel Ghadaffi has unsuccessfully attempted to influence various African nations to acknowledge him leader of an African Union. The reason for his repeated rejections for this position was due to his reputation for being a treacherous individual. (Carney 2003)

Therefore, for these same African nations, who for over three decades rejected Ghadaffi to lead them, to all of a sudden do an about-face and elect him leader of an African union for his having made oil available to the west suggests another motive.

This being the case, one motive that appears is that since many African nations are indebted to western nations and the World Bank, and rely on these entities for various levels of assistance, African leaders could have changed their votes in favor of Ghadaffi as their head in exchange for more lenient terms on their debts.

And if so, with Colonel Ghadaffi now head of an African Union and with Daniel 11:42 depicting the antichrist having dominion over several countries, it then appears that Colonel Ghadaffi has also met this criterion for the antichrist.

In addition, as Colonel Ghadaffi's new status as head of an African Union has been officiated in conjunction with authority from the first beast having negotiated with African leaders for their votes, the criterion in Revelation 13:12 of the antichrist exercising full authority from the first beast also appears to have been met.

However, as Revelation 13:12 also describes the first beast's mortal wound having been healed, indicating a full recovery from an economic depression that in 2009 has yet to be officially declared such, it then appears the authority from the beast that propelled Colonel Ghadaffi into office over an African Union in February 2009 does not constitute the authority that will be issued to the antichrist by the beast in Rev. 13:5, 7, and 12.

Being such, the next step is in assessing further data in relation with the beast's mortal wound in order to see how and when the antichrist's authority will be issued.

As Daniel 8:8–9 describes, the prominent horn of the he-goat that attacks and conquers Media and Persia (Daniel 8:20) will be broken into four good-sized horns, one of which the antichrist will form an alliance with and grow very large; once these events occur, the antichrist's 2,300-day reign will commence (Daniel 8:14). This data would indicate that, despite Colonel Ghadaffi having made Libya's oil reserves available in 2008 that aided in stabilizing the beasts economies throughout 2009, this aid will nonetheless be insufficient in averting the 2009 global recession from turning into a 2010-and-onward global depression that, within the United States, will create greater economic disparity between states until ultimately resulting in the fifty United States seceding into four separate unions (four horns), one of which the antichrist will then form an alliance with, as described in Daniel 8:9.

Once this alliance is formed the antichrist will then uproot three of the beast's ten horns (Daniel 7:8), at which time the antichrist will then constitute an eighth horn of the beast at this time (as ten horns minus three horns plus the antichrist's horn will then equal eight horns).

When these events take place, the world's other socioeconomic systems, described as separate entities from the fourth beast in Daniel 7:3–7 (leopard, bear, and lion), will then be united to the primary beast in a single global socioeconomic endeavor, as depicted in Rev. 13:1–2.

Despite, however, that most of the world's nations today appear to meet this criterion representing a loosely unified socioeconomic entity, with the commencement of the antichrist's 2,300 days and nights contingent upon his forming an alliance with one of the four new horns that will emerge from the seceded fifty contiguous United States, under the current status of allegiance between the United

States and the nation of Israel such an allegiance between the US and the nation of Libya would constitute at least a conflict of interest, and at worst treason against the land of Israel.

Support for this latter perspective appears when Isaiah 33:1 describes: "Alas for you, devastator! you who have not been devastated yourself; you traitor, whom they have not betrayed! When you have ceased to devastate, you shall be devastated yourself; and when you have ended your traitorous deeds, you shall be betrayed yourself."

With this scripture describing treason from an ally to the land of Israel; although many theologians have assumed this scripture refers to an event approximately 100 years after Isaiah in the 6th century BC when Nebuchadnezzar, king of Babylon and the Chaldeans, would invade and conquer the land of Israel, while this invasion would fit the description of a devastator, the description of Nebuchadnezzar and the Chaldeans as allied with the land of Zion prior to its having been conquered does not apply, and would therefore not constitute the traitor described in Isaiah 33:1.

Being such, and as much of Isaiah pertains to the final tribulation period, Isaiah 33:1 would then likely pertain to an ally with the state of Israel today. And in conjunction with the description of a land that devastates, the US currently best fits all the criteria for this profile.

Isaiah 21:1–2 also states: "A message concerning the desert of the west. As whirlwinds in the south-land sweep on, so it comes from the desert, the land of terror. A harsh vision is declared to me; the traitor deals treacherously, and the destroyer demolishes…"

With the exception of whirlwinds and desert, were the US to form an alliance with the antichrist, the description of a land of terror, described as a treacherous traitor that destroys and demolishes, would then apply.

However, as the descriptions of whirlwinds and a desert land appear to conflict with the US representing this entity, we then need further data as to what and/or when this description is in reference to.

As Isaiah 28:19–20, in association with these events in regards to the land of Israel, relates:

> As often as it passes through, it will carry you away, for morning by morning will it pass, by day and by night. It will be unmixed terror to understand the message. For the bed is too short to stretch one's self upon it and the covering too narrow for him to wrap himself in it.

With Isaiah 28:19–20 referring to daily air raids upon the land of Israel of which she is presented as incapable of retaliating against, indicating a vastly superior force than that of the Israeli military, and with the description in Isaiah 33:1 of a traitor hypothetically pertaining to the US as responsible for this event, the current status quo between these two nations would have to undergo extreme change in order for this type of scenario to come about.

Therefore, as the description of whirlwinds and desert in Isaiah 21:1–2 indicates that severe environmental changes will also have to occur, and with such changes affecting agricultural output in the United States to the point where its current status as a major contributor to the world's food resources would cease, requiring it to import greater quantities of sustenance for its own people, the daily air raids on the land of Israel by one of the four horns of a seceded United States that will form an alliance with the antichrist would then appear to be in exchange for said sustenance from the antichrist.

As this indicates that not only the environmental status of the United States will be affected, but that of the entire world; further scientific and apocalyptic data will then provide greater insight as to how these events will come about.

The Antichrist's Rise

While being head of an African Union meets the criterion of the antichrist having dominion over several countries, as described in Daniel 11:42; as the next passage in Daniel 11:43 describes Egypt's treasures, gold, silver, and valuables coming under the antichrists control, we see what appears to be a redundancy in describing Egypt's treasures along with its gold, silver, and valuables coming under the antichrist's control.

Assuming a redundancy was not being depicted when mentioning Egypt's treasures, then along with Egypt's limited reserves of gold, silver, and other precious commodities, Egypt's treasures would represent something other than what is commonly associated with treasure.

This being the case, when Revelation 13:11 describes the second beast—the antichrist —emerging from the land (indicating the antichrist's supremacy will come from the land); although having made Libya's oil available to the west has propelled Colonel Ghadaffi to become head of an African Union, as these nations currently represent a nominal increase in Ghadaffi's stature, a rise to global prominence would indicate this increase in stature will derive from another source other than the oil the nation of Libya currently provides to the west.

But as the terrains of the African Union from which the antichrist is to rise to worldwide prominence consist primarily of deserts today, this hypothetical scenario appears somewhat absurd. This perception, however, represents the current status quo within these nations, which according to various data is about to change.

When Libya's oil reserves were opened to the west in 2008, Colonel Ghadaffi decided he would use the billions of dollars realized to purchase various items, including a nuclear power reactor and a desalination plant that, when placed in tandem, will produce great quantities of potable water. (Omestead 2007)

And as one of Ghadaffi's long-held ambitions has been that of a green Libya, he intends to use the enormous quantities of potable water a nuclear-powered desalination plant will produce to irrigate many currently arid but fertile terrains within Libya that in turn will provide Libyans with greater self-sufficiency in feeding themselves. ("The Arab World" 1973)

And as Daniel 11:24 describes the acquisition of fertile provinces as one of the antichrist's primary endeavors; when Rev. 13:11 describes the second beast rising from the earth; in an apocalyptic world where food resources will have become increasingly scarce, the antichrist's rise to world prominence indicates he will do so with an excess of produce that will allow him to export food staples while few other nations at this time, if any, will be able to export food. This will then appear somewhat comparable to the global famine in Genesis 41–45, where the world of the time had to travel to Egypt for food. But unlike the famine in Genesis 41–45 that was brought about by God and/or natural causes, this new global famine will be the result of desertification brought about by global warming.

Micah 7:13

"Yet the earth shall become a waste on account of her inhabitants, because of the fruits of their works."

And while some may anticipate this type of environmental scenario being decades into the distant future, one recent example of global warming having impacted a major food contributor to the worlds food resources negatively was seen in Australia in 2008, where, due to severe drought conditions having persisted for several years, rice production, which requires large quantities of irrigation, was reduced by 98 percent—from 1.2 million metric tons to 18,000 metric tons—resulting in a significant increase in malnutrition and starvation in many of the world's poorer nations. (Walsh 2008)

Another recent example of global warming, not as severe as that seen in Australia, but with the prospect of becoming just as bad, if not worse, has been the ongoing drought in the western United States, where for the last several years snow accumulations in the higher elevations of mountain regions have been declining annually. As this form of precipitation accounts for nearly 80 percent of many western states' potable water, the results have been increasing deprivation of the water necessary to produce harvests comparable with those in prior years.

And while prices for fruits and vegetables from these areas have remained fairly stable where demand has not significantly exceeded supply, declining harvest productions from these areas in the future will inevitably see a substantial increase in cost for these produce.

Therefore, as global warming and desertification will continue to decrease agricultural outputs from many of the world's food exporting nations, many poorer nations that cannot afford to purchase food and depend on certain levels of assistance from food exporting nations will find it increasingly difficult, if not impossible, in the near future to acquire sufficient sustenance from these sources. And as many of these nations will then quickly exhaust all their means to acquire food from whatever source is available, global mass starvation will then ensue on levels not seen in recorded history.

But, as the nation of Libya will have an excess of food production when the global famine appears, with Daniel 11:43 describing the Ethiopians in the antichrist's retinue during this time, it then appears this will be the result of the Ethiopians having placed themselves in servitude to the antichrist in exchange for sustenance.

And with Daniel 11:43 also describing Egypt's *treasures*, as well as gold, silver, and other valuables, coming under the antichrist's control, it would appear that after Egypt will have exhausted its gold, silver, and other valuables reserves in exchange for food with the antichrist, Egypt will then relinquish its treasures, representing its fertile provinces, to the antichrist. The reason for this will be that, although terrains along the Nile are among the most fertile and productive today, during the days of apocalypse the Nile will become worthless. This is described in Isaiah 19:5–7:

"The waters of the sea will be dried up, and the river will run empty and be dried up. The rivers will become foul, and the streams of Egypt will decrease and dry up; the reeds and rushes will rot away. The meadows alongside the river and the mouth of the river and all the seeded fields bordering on the river will be dried up, blown away; they shall be no more."

With this outcome looming for Egypt's Nile, and with the Egyptians having no alternate means of irrigation when this occurs; relinquishing Egypt's treasures—its fertile provinces—along the dried-up Nile to Ghadaffi, who will have access to large quantities of potable water from his desalination plant(s), will then make more sense than starving to many Egyptians.

Furthermore, as Egypt coming under the control of the antichrist in Daniel 8:9 is described in conjunction with his growing larger by expanding "...southward, eastward, and toward the Glory land," with his expansion towards the Glory land constituting the time when he will stand at the temple in Jerusalem representing the commencement of the 42 month tribulation period, described in Daniel 9:27 as the middle of the week in his 2,300 day reign; these events then appear precipitated by the prevailing dire environmental conditions of the period.

And as the antichrist will have the resources through his desalination plants to lessen famine conditions, the primary beast will then grant the antichrist full authority to annex Egypt's fertile provinces and place these into production.

The next issue this raises is that even if Libya's and Egypt's fertile terrains were to produce abundant quantities of food that would suffice in providing various nations with sustenance, to supply 6.6 billion people with sufficient sustenance during a global famine would require more fertile provinces than from these two nations.

Being such, as a southward expansion is included in Daniel 8:9 with the description of the antichrist becoming larger; one extremely fertile province laying just south of Libya is in the nation of Chad, in a region of the eastern Sahel known as the Bodele Valley depression (currently an arid and mostly uncultivated terrain).

One problem, however, is that while this fertile terrain, if it were extensively irrigated, would yield great quantities of produce, doing so would produce various environmental repercussions.

In 2005, when the Amazon basin experienced its greatest drought on record, the continental United States experienced various meteorological phenomena, which included a significant increase in tornado activity.

And while the increased meteorological activity in the US was the result of the Amazon's severe drought, the drought in the Amazon was the result of global warming.

You may now be asking: what does this have to do with the Bodele Valley and its environmental status with the earth?

Annually, winds blowing across the Bodele carry approximately 50 million tons of nutrient rich microorganism dust—diatoms—to the Amazon Basin, without which the Amazon would become an arid landscape in a short period of time. (Manning 2006)

And as the dust from the Bodele to the Amazon is contingent upon its arid status allowing it to become airborne; if the Bodele were to become irrigated for agricultural purposes, the Bodele's dust would soon cease to become airborne, causing the Amazon to become arid with characteristics similar to the 2005 drought, thereby causing within the US meteorological events similar to those that occurred in 2005.

However, as the rains that returned to the Amazon in 2006 resulted in meteorological events in the US returning to normal levels, were the Bodele to be irrigated on an annual basis and the Bodele's aerosol of nutrients to remain grounded, the Amazon would continue to deteriorate, further increasing global warming that would further affect meteorological changes.

And while the loss of the Amazonian rain forests would pose a great environmental catastrophe, it would be only one of several environmental catastrophes that would result were the Sahel's winds to cease transporting the Bodele's dusts.

As 50 million tons of the Bodele's diatoms annually traverse the Atlantic Ocean to fertilize the Amazon's rain forests, approximately 140 million tons of it falls into the Atlantic Ocean that in turn becomes the primary food source for numerous microscopic marine species (e.g. plankton).

Being such, any sizable depletion of the Bodele's nutrients falling into the Atlantic Ocean would result in a significant depletion in plankton, which in turn would climb the food chain until ultimately eliminating the Atlantic Ocean as a viable source of sustenance for mankind.

Besides falling on the Amazon and into the Atlantic Ocean, the Bodele's dusts also carry over to fall on the North American continent; unfortunately these quantities are mostly unknown, and therefore, remain somewhat speculative as to what level of benefit US soils derive annually through this means of fertilization.

One possible means, however, in assessing what affects would occur in the US should the Bodele's diatoms decrease in quantity is through historical meteorological data. And as meteorological data for the Sahel during the 1920s–1930s indicates it having been less arid than today, lesser quantities of the Bodele's dusts would have been airlifted into the atmosphere than in drier years. And as the US during the 1930s experienced the dust bowl event, diminished quantities of the Bodele's dusts may have hastened this event.

In which case, should the Bodele reach similarly wet conditions as those in the 1920s—either naturally or through manmade irrigation—another series of dust bowls in the US could result that would then severely impede agricultural production in the US as it did during the 1930s.

These results, however, assume hygroscopic levels on the Sahel would not exceed those of the 1920s and 1930s, where the amount of Bodele's diatoms becoming airborne may have diminished by as much as 10 percent from levels seen today and, therefore, were still sufficient to keep the Amazon green, the Atlantic Ocean marine life in balance, and the US's soils fertilized to a certain degree, despite the dust bowl.

If, however, conditions on the Bodele were to become significantly wetter than those recorded for the 1920s and 1930s, that would result in significantly greater decrease of the Bodele's diatoms being airlifted and transported west; such ramifications might only be speculated upon, as no recorded historical meteorological data for the Bodele being considerably wetter than today exists.

However, while it is true that no recorded data for such an event exist, there are various other means the sciences utilize to look in on events that transpired prior to recorded history.

One of these means is through geology (the study of the earth's minerals and composites), which over the years has led the sciences to numerous discoveries leading all the way back to the earth's inception over 4.5 billion years ago.

One recent geologic discovery comes from an area in the Delaware peninsula, where soil accumulations in excess of one foot were deposited within less than one thousand years, from approximately 11-10 thousand years ago (11-10 KYA), which could only have occurred if high wind velocities were regular meteorological events.

This geological data led to another scientific discovery not directly related with geology. Although numerous hypotheses exist as to why many large mammalian species went extinct during the late Pleistocene12-10 KYA, regular high wind speeds 11-10 KYA would have severely hindered the growth of plant life at that time, and as a result, large herbivores not finding sufficient plant growth would have significantly diminished in number, with some herbivore species going altogether extinct. And as many of the larger predatory species that fed on herbivores would have found fewer herbivores to feed upon, many predatory species would also have diminished in number, with some going altogether extinct.

While some scientists have speculated the high wind speeds 11-10 KYA were the result of the last glaciation event coming to a close, as many of the large mammalian species that went extinct 11-10 KYA had survived through numerous glacial and interglacial events over many hundreds of thousands of years (and in some species' cases, millions of years), another glacial event coming to a close would be insufficient to explain these extinctions—or the high wind speeds over the Eastern sea board of the United States that appeared simultaneously with these extinctions.

Therefore, in addition to the last glaciation event coming to a close, there would had to have been an additional factor or factors that precipitated the high wind velocities that in all likelihood caused the extinctions of numerous species that had survived multiple glacial and interglacial events.

One such factor was that as the last glacial event was receding north, Lake Agassiz, an immense glacial lake located in the center of North America and covering an area larger than any lake in the world today, had formed. At its largest, it was larger than the state of California when its contents drained into the Atlantic Ocean, causing what many scientists believe was the ocean's primary current, the Great Ocean Conveyor, to cease flowing.

In turn, this precipitated a temporary 1,300-year return to glacial-like temperatures in an event known as the Younger Dryas from about 12,800 to 11,500 years ago. Once the Younger Dryas came to a close and temperatures began to warm again, events not common with glacial and interglacial closings over the previous 500,000 years had transpired.

An article on Africa in the *Los Angeles Times*, August 15, 2008; titled: "Archaeologists get a glimpse of life in a Sahara Eden" indicates that, where the Sahara had been a desert for untold millennia, about 12,000 years ago "….a faint wobble in Earth's orbit, and some other factors, caused Africa's seasonal monsoons to shift slightly north, bringing rains to the Sahara and greening it from Egypt in the east to Mauritania in the west."

With this being the case, as the Sahara was becoming green starting about 12,000 years ago, the Bodele's diatoms would not have been airborne; as a result the Atlantic Ocean, the Amazon, and the North American continent would have experienced the affects of such.

One of these effects would have been the Amazon exchanging topographical characteristics with the Sahara. And with the Amazon becoming an arid landscape11-10 KYA, the North American continent would have experienced greater meteorological events than those that resulted from the 2005 drought in the Amazon, thereby corroborating the high wind velocity data for the Delaware peninsula 11–10 KYA.

Therefore, with these types of environmental repercussions likely should the Bodele's dusts cease from becoming airborne, it would appear maintaining the Bodele Valley's current status would be in everyone's best interest.

And so it would appear, except that with a global famine slated to coincide with the reign of the antichrist, indicating agricultural production worldwide will change drastically from its current status, the most likely cause will be from global warming having increased hygroscopic levels in the Bodele, preventing its diatoms from becoming airborne and causing an environmental domino cascade that will not only severely curtail agricultural production from the United States but will severely affect agricultural output from the rest of the North and South American continents as well.

And as three of the world's four leading food-exporting nations are located in the Americas (the US, Canada, and Argentina), depleting agricultural harvests from the Americas will then foster the global famine associated with the days of tribulation.

In which case, and at which time, as the world's inhabitants will be experiencing significantly greater levels of starvation and while the Bodele Valley experiences transformation from its current status of arid landscape to fertile valley, rather than let the world experience greater levels of starvation than necessary, the beast will authorize the antichrist to take control of several fertile provinces in Northern

Africa and place them into agricultural production.

One question this prospect raises is that, even if the antichrist will represent a new member (the little horn) in association with the beast (the G-7), why will the beast let the antichrist control such a strategic resource?

Besides the fact that the antichrist will have the capacity to irrigate various fertile terrains that would be left unproductive without water provided from his desalination plants, these fertile terrains, including the Bodele valley, will not suffice in feeding 6.6 billion people. In which case, it then appears this will precipitate the beast's "think tanks" into initiating the genocides described in the book of Revelation through their new member, the antichrist.

By doing so, rather than take direct control of the world's new bread basket in northern Africa and having to distribute meager survival portions of sustenance to the earth's 6.6 billion inhabitants, the beast will instead, under the guise of complying with the sovereign nation providing sustenance to the world (Libya), authorize the antichrist to take control of these fertile provinces and initiate the mark of the beast, thereby eliminating sharing sustenance with the anticipated billions of individuals who will refuse to receive the beast's mark while exonerating itself to the world from directly having to initiate genocidal policies.

In addition, as extreme famine conditions will prevail, there will be few among the faithless that receive the mark of the beast who will object to a genocidal policy against those who will refuse the mark of the beast, as it will mean their receiving those individuals' portion of sustenance.

And while such a scenario today appears surreal, keep in mind that by the time a global famine commences under the fourth seal the first three seals will have achieved a global state of anarchy where most of the world's inhabitants will be at a point eagerly awaiting any potentially remedying policy, including looking away from the fate of those who will refuse to receive the mark of the beast.

In further support of this conjecture, as the first three seals' events describe anarchy along with an economic depression that will leave most individuals unemployed and without means to purchase sustenance, with Rev. 13:17 describing those who will receive the mark permitted to conduct transactions, the mark of the beast then appears as a type of welfare system that will allow a certain stipend for the purchase of basics and other commodities, despite massive unemployment. And if so, the deaths of many of those who refuse the mark of the beast will appear more as suicide rather than genocide and therefore will not appear as an immoral act by those who will receive the mark of the beast.

However, as either the name or number of the beast on one's hand or forehead is strictly forbidden in the book of Revelation (primarily for the hedonistic lifestyle it will promote), those who receive the mark of the beast will be deemed culpable for the deaths of those who die for refusing the mark of the beast under the fourth and fifth seals (Rev. 16:5–6), as the true motive for keeping silent will be to attain the share of food of those who refuse the mark of the beast; with these acts constituting faithlessness towards God, the definition of the word "antichrist"—aka atheist—will then apply to those who receive the mark of the beast.

This, however, raises a couple of issues, the first being that in 2009 only about 14 percent of individuals worldwide declared themselves as atheists; and if according to Revelation 6:8 the majority of those who will not accept the mark of the beast are killed, representing 25 percent of the earth's inhabitants, the approximate remaining 75 percent of mankind would then be comprised of atheists/antichrists, thereby conflicting with current statistics. (Kosmin 2008)

Moreover, with Christianity representing approximately 33 percent of the world population in 2009, even if everyone other than those claiming affiliation with Christianity were to receive the mark of the beast, in order for 75 percent of mankind to receive the mark of the beast, approximately one fourth of Christians today will receive the mark of the beast. ("Religions" 2009)

Therefore, as this represents a great falling away among many who currently claim faith in God, including Christians, this falling away from faith will be the direct result of the Lords intervention. This is described in Hebrews 12:26–27 where He states: "Once more I will shake, not only the earth but heaven as well...indicating the final removal of everything shaken-created things, so that the unshaken things may remain."

And as Hebrews 12:26–27 describes a global change in attitude from faith in God towards atheism, it indicates that while approximately 85 percent of the world currently profess faith in a deity of some sort, as the majority of these faiths have been contingent upon experiencing stability in relatively good times, when the global economy deteriorates and events become extremely dire, most, with the exception of about 25 percent of mankind, will then lose their faith in God.

The primary reason for this great falling away from faith in God will be due to the fact that most individuals' faiths today are not backed by any knowledge on the Word of God but instead rely on ritualistic forms of piety, and with no true foundation to base their faiths upon, those created forms of faith will not stand during turbulent times.

Therefore, with approximately an additional 61 percent of the world's populace scheduled to join the current 14 percent of declared atheists in receiving the mark of the beast, among the first to be shaken out will be those professing faith in creeds other than Christianity, who without the Word warning against receiving the mark of the beast will readily accept the mark of the beast.

But also, as mentioned previously, with Christians currently representing approximately 33 percent of the world's populace, in order for 75 percent of the world to fall away and receive the mark of the beast, at least several hundred million currently professing themselves as Christians will be among those receiving the mark of the beast.

Of these Christian affiliates, those who expect a rapture of their bodies and souls prior to when Revelation 6:7–11 clearly describes that 25 percent of the earth's inhabitants who will not receive the mark of the beast under the fourth and fifth seals timeframes are to be killed, when finding themselves under these conditions, will then be among those falling away from the faith for having trusted a fallacy instead of scripture.

And with the reason for these individuals' shakeout being their trust in a myth instead of God's word, this group represents "the seed that falls on the road or on the bedrock that have no root" (the Word) who quickly fall away under tribulation. (Luke 8:5, 6, 11–13)

In conjunction with no root (the Word) that will fool many into receiving the mark of the beast, other factors that will cause many to fall away from faith in God will be various misnomers associated with the mark of the beast.

Having only recently established from the earliest scrolls that the antichrist's number is 616 and not 666, with his name corresponding with his number (Rev. 13:17), individuals unaware of this data that see a name or number corresponding with one other than 666 will have little compunction in receiving such a mark.

Furthermore, although the number of the beast relates directly to the number of a man (Rev. 13:18), as the antichrist will represent one of the primary beast's members, the beast's name and number the antichrist will compel the world to have placed on their hands will reference his affiliation with the primary beast. And if so, those who expect to see a number in direct reference to the antichrist and instead see reference to an association with a global socioeconomic system they do not believe represents the mark of the antichrist: some will then accept this mark.

And while it may appear excessive to some that those who accept the mark of the beast due to the aforementioned erroneous interpretations should receive the repercussions Rev. 14:9–11 describes will befall all who accept the mark of the beast, these repercussions will be the result of the numerous immoral actions those who will receive the mark of the beast will undertake, which will include looking the other way from the fate of those refusing the mark of the beast in order to attain a greater share of sustenance for themselves.

And as those who will receive the mark of the beast will represent antichrists (aka atheists) and by definition are not spiritual-minded but natural-minded, these individuals will have as their primary instinct their own physical pleasure, which naturally brings about immoral attitudes. In which case, without a spiritual morality in ones being brought about by faith, the moral behavior exemplified among the faithless is produced by laws, rules, and regulations that castigate various immoral acts.

In regards to the definition of immorality, although its primary connotation is often associated with sexual immorality, the broader definition of the term is that of an incorrect manner of thinking resulting in an incorrect manner of living, which the New Testament of the Bible describes as brought about by idolatry.

Idolatry

When idolatry is mentioned, it often connotes images of icons made of wood, stone, clay, metal, etc., to which less enlightened individuals in the past as well as in the present paid homage to. And while this form of idolatry is the type often depicted in the Old Testament, in the New Testament, when idolatry is described, it is usually in reference to material goods that individuals pursue with a passion.

The New Webster Encyclopedic Dictionary (1969) describes this form of idolatry as "…any person or thing on which we strongly set our affections; that to which we are excessively, often improperly, attached."

Therefore, with an improper attachment of one's affections towards things (materialism) constituting the primary definition of idolatry, in today's modern society where technology (described as magic arts in Rev, 9:21, 18:23, and 21:8) provides ever-increasing amounts of material goods/idols, an ever-increasing insatiable desire (described as wantonness in Rev. 18:3 and 9) to possess more of these idols will have transformed mankind into an idolistic/immoral society when the days of apocalypse arrive.

While some may argue that being materialistic is benign and does not lead to immoral behavior, the Bible, on the other hand, in Ephesians 5:5 and Colossians 3:5, describes materialistic idolatry as something to steer clear of.

One extreme example of immorality brought about by materialistic idolatry is described in Revelation 18:3–7, where "Babylon the Great," who for "her abundant wantonness" (insatiable desires) "lives in sensuality" (a state of subjection to the appetites) and as a result is deemed responsible for all the world's atrocities in Rev. 17:5 and 18:24.

While this sounds like a lot of culpability to have assessed an entity for simply enjoying a sensual lifestyle, when Rev. 14:8, 17:2, and 18:3 describe the inhabitants of the earth having become intoxicated (elated to enthusiasm, frenzy, or madness) with the wine of her passionate immorality (materialism), it indicates that while the nations of the earth partake in Babylon the Great's sensuous lifestyle they will also undertake similar immoral policies as Babylon the Great, which will lead to thefts, murders, and all the earth's other abominations described in Rev. 9:21 and 17:5.

In which case, as Babylon the Great will be the initiator of these policies, the whole of these acts will then justifiably be attributed to her. And as these events are to coincide when environmental conditions on the earth will have ushered in the global famine, where lawlessness and immorality prevail, it becomes easier to realize the immoral approach the beast's members will initiate with the beast's mark through their new member—the antichrist—while anticipating the elimination of billions of individuals who will refuse to accept the mark of the beast.

While this depiction continues to remain somewhat surreal today with insufficient cause for the world's enlightened nations to enact genocidal policies–even if through an accomplice; when Mark 13:19 says, "for the misery of those days will be such as never was since the beginning of God's creation until now, neither ever will be"; with all of earth's inhabitants experiencing extreme anguish as these events unfold, when a new global welfare system is initiated promising to alleviate the misery of those days through compliance with a mark on one's hand or forehead, such a scenario does not appear that outlandish.

Those who join, however, soon appear in severe conflict with those who will not join; as this is described in Mark 13:12–13: "Brother will hand over brother for death, and father will hand over son; children will rise against their parents and have them put to death, and you will be hated by every one, because of My name. But whoever perseveres to the end will be saved."

As those who will persevere unto the end represent those with sufficient faith to persist until their own demise, the hatred directed towards these individuals will be due to jealousy from those who will not persevere to see their own demise and will therefore receive the mark of the beast.

While jealousy may seem an insufficient motive to have family members turning in other family members for execution, Matthew 24:9–10 describes the same events as those described in Mark chapter 13:

Then they will hand you over to be persecuted and they will kill you, and you will be hated by all the nations on account of My name. Many will then fall away and will betray one another and hate one another.

With the people who will be persecuted on account of His name referring to those individuals who will maintain faith in the Lord's name, while those betraying and hating these individuals, will be those who fall away due to their lack of faith; jealousy then appears as the cause described.

And as those who fall away will constitute those having insufficient faith in seeing their own demise, the hatred they will have towards those with the Lord's name (that will include family members) represents those having sufficient faith who will refuse the mark of the beast, even to the point of death.

Therefore, with 25 percent of mankind who will be killed refusing the mark of the beast constituting events under the fourth and fifth seals in association with the fourth rider of the Apocalypse (Rev. 6:8–9), when Matthew 24:15–16 says, "When you, therefore, see the desolating abomination mentioned by the Prophet Daniel, set up in the holy place—let the reader take note of this—then those in Judea should flee to the mountains," the desolating abomination appears as another metaphor for the fourth rider—the antichrist.

And with the desolating abomination/the antichrist described in the holy place (Matthew 24:15–16), sanctuary (Daniel 8:13), and where it should not be (Mark 13:14), at which time those in Judea should then flee to the mountains, 2 Thessalonians 2:3–4 further defines these descriptions as representing the temple of God, where the antichrist will appear:

> "….for the apostasy is to come first, and the man of sin is to be revealed, the one doomed to hell, the adversary who opposes and rises up against every so-called god and what is worshipped, so that he seats himself in the temple of God with the claim that he himself is God."

One dilemma the antichrist standing in the temple of God currently poses is the assumption many theologians have that the temple in reference is the Judaic temple of Solomon where the Wailing Wall stands, which will need to be rebuilt in order for the antichrist to make his appearance there.

If this assumption were correct, however, it would indicate that the forces who will occupy Jerusalem forty-two months after it is destroyed (in all likelihood by the Palestinians and other Muslim factions with whom the nation of Israel has been in conflict with for decades) would voluntarily rebuild Solomon's Judaic temple. (Luke 21:24) (Rev. 11:2)

As this is an unlikely scenario, a more plausible outcome might be that after Jerusalem is leveled the temple to be rebuilt by the Gentiles will be the Muslim Dome of the Rock where the original first Judaic temple stood.

Another issue this raises is the assumption many believe, that the beast's number will be in association with the antichrist's appearance in God's temple in Jerusalem. If this were so, however, with the antichrist's number 616 representing a chronological point in time between 2008 and 2012, the destruction and rebuilding of Jerusalem would have to occur in the next couple of years in order for the antichrist to seat himself in the rebuilt temple of God in Jerusalem by 2012.

And while not impossible, as events under the third seal indicating a world working for basic sustenance in lieu of monetary gain have yet to be realized, a rapid progression of the third seal's events would also have to occur in order for the fourth seal's events to commence by 2012.

Therefore, while it is possible that the antichrist's number 616 will directly relate with his appearance at God's temple in Jerusalem by 2012, the more likely scenario is that it will commemorate the 2008 affiliation between the antichrist and the beast, which will be enacted upon when the antichrist enters Jerusalem and seats himself in the rebuilt temple of God, which may or may not occur as early as 2012.

But when the antichrist does appear at the rebuilt temple in Jerusalem; with Daniel 9:27 stating, "In a week he shall make the covenant to prevail with many..." that describes the antichrist's new world order with the beast as seven years, "...and in the middle of the week he will cause sacrifice and offering to cease," indicating that in the middle of the antichrist's seven-year reign with the beast he will then appear at the temple in Jerusalem where he will initiate the mark of the beast; the 3.5 years of tribulation period for the Lord's people, described as forty-two months in Daniel 12:7 and Revelation 11:2 and 13:5, and as 1,290 days in Daniel 12:11, will then commence. After this Daniel 9:27 continues to describe: "Then on a wing of horrors shall a desolator come to bring ruin until a fully determined end comes down on the desolation." With this description indicating that, after Jerusalem has been devastated and the temple rebuilt and the antichrist makes his appearance there, a desolating air force will then bring ruin to the rest of the land of Israel, this description then appears strikingly similar with the description in Isaiah 28:19–20: "As often as it passes through, it will carry you away, for morning by morning will it pass, by day and by night. It will be unmixed terror to understand the message. For the bed is too short to stretch one's self upon it and the covering too narrow to wrap himself in it."

With the bed too short to stretch one's self upon it describing Israel's north-to-south borders too short to run far, the covering too narrow to wrap himself in it describes Israel's east-to-west borders as too narrow to provide cover.

While this will be the fate for almost all who are living in the land of Israel at this time, as the mark of the beast will be initiated in conjunction with this event; over the next forty-two months one fourth of the earth's populace constituting the Lord's people will also be killed.

At the conclusion of the tribulation period of the Lord's people, Daniel 12:12 quotes: "Blessed is the expectant one who attains 1,335 days."

As this blessing indicates this occurring forty-five days after the tribulation associated with the Lord's people has concluded, many theologians have assumed this blessing to be in association with the return of the Lord Jesus.

However, if this were the case, as events constituting the tribulation for the Lord's people are represented under the fourth and fifth seals, events under the sixth and seventh seals would have to conclude within a forty-five-day period in order for this hypothesis to be valid.

Furthermore, by having knowledge of when the tribulation commenced, if the Lord Jesus were to return 1,335 days after it had commenced, scripture declaring the Lord's return "will come like a thief when no one will expect Him" (Matthew 24:44; 1 Thessalonians 5:2; Luke 12:40; Rev. 16:15) would be invalid, as His approximate return would be realized.

Therefore, as these events do not represent the end but do represent a major transition from under the fourth and fifth seals to those under the sixth seal, various scripture provide further data in relation with these events.

When Isaiah 60:1–3 describes a dawning radiance coming upon the Lord's people after their having gone through a period of tribulation during the final days, the dawning radiance appears as an analogy to the blessing on day 1,335.

And while this dawning radiance is bestowed upon the Lord's people, Isaiah 60:2 says, "For behold, darkness shall cover the earth and a dark cloud the nations...." indicating the beast's and antichrist's system will be in the process of collapse at the end of the antichrists 2,300-day reign in association with the beast.

Despite that the beast and antichrist's system will be in the process of collapse/darkness, once the blessing of dawning radiance is bestowed upon the Lord's people, Isaiah 60:4 then describes the Lord's people being transported to the land of Israel, which Isaiah 49:22–23 and 66:20 elaborate in greater detail—with the kings of the earth personally involving themselves in these individuals' transport.

And with the kings of the earth personally involving themselves in the transport of individuals who for the previous forty-two months had been set aside for genocide, it then indicates the blessing of dawning radiance will be one that will make a notable impression on the world's inhabitants.

This is corroborated in Isaiah 62:2: "The nations shall behold your deliverance and all the kings your glory. You shall be called by a new name, which the mouth of the Lord shall bestow."

With the latter part of Isaiah 62:2 mentioning a new name bestowed on the Lord's people; Isaiah 65:13–15 elaborates further on who these people with a new name are, and who they are not:

> Therefore thus says the Lord God, "Behold My servants shall eat, but you shall be hungry; take note, My servants shall drink, but you shall be thirsty; observe, My servants shall rejoice, but you shall be put to shame; mark well, My servants shall sing for gladness of heart, but you shall cry out for sorrow of heart and shall wail for anguish of soul. You shall leave your name for a curse to My chosen ones; the Lord God shall slay you; but His servants shall be called by another name."

As to who will leave their name to the Lord's chosen ones; it appears that "Jew" would be the name in reference.

In which case, when Luke 21:32, Mark 13:30, and Matthew 24:34 quote Jesus stating: "I assure you that all this will happen before this generation passes away," the generation who will not pass away before the end comes refers to those who will not have received the mark of the beast, have survived the tribulation under the fourth and fifth seals' timeframes, have received the blessing of dawning radiance on day 1,335, and have been transported by the world's rulers to the land of Zion.

From this data, we further realize that the premise of the Jew returning to the land of Israel in 1948 as representing the generation that will not pass away before the return of the Lord is erroneous, and that the Jew in reference is not to a blood race of individuals but instead—as described in Romans 10:14–21 represents those with faith in the Lord Jesus. This is supported by Romans 11:1–4, where it describes only 7,000 Jews of blood heritage will be among those with faith in the Lord Jesus who are saved in the land of Israel during the final days.

Romans 9:25-27 further states:

So too he says in Hosea, "I will call those who were not My people, 'My people,' and her who was not loved, 'My beloved,' and in the place where it was said to them, 'You are not My people,' there they will be called sons of the living God."

Isaiah, too, exclaims regarding Israel,

"Even though the number of Israel's sons were as the sand of the sea, only a remnant will be saved."

And in reference to Isaiah 65:1–2, Romans 10:20–21 states:

"….I have been found by those who did not seek Me; I have shown Myself to those who did not ask for Me." But concerning Israel He says, "All day long I have held out My hands to a disobedient and rebellious people."

Galatians 3:6–7 also confirms the status of those who are sons of Abraham as those of faith. And of those who believe in Christ, Galatians 3:28 says, "There is neither Jew nor Greek, there is neither slave nor freeman, there is neither male nor female, because you are all one in Christ Jesus."

Whereas those who depend on works of the Law for their righteousness Galatians 3:10 describes as living under a curse, for it is written, "Cursed is everyone who does not abide by all that is written in the book of the Law so as to do it."

Therefore, realizing that those the Lord will accept will be those with faith in Him while those currently referred to as Jews He will slay, some may now be under the impression that the Jews in reference represent the Jews in the land of Israel. The problem with this assessment, however, is that the land of Israel will have been devastated over the last forty-two months, with most of its Judaic populace already killed, when those with faith in the Lord commence appearing in the land of Israel.

In which case, as the blessing of dawning radiance bestowed on day 1,335 will commence the return of the Lord's people to the devastated land of Israel, at which time the annihilation of the Jewish race as described in Isaiah 65:13–15 will coincide, these verses then describe the additional annihilation of the entire global Jewish race that will commence within the sixth seal's timeframe.

Corroboration of this outcome appears with Revelation 9:18 describing one third of the earth's inhabitants to be killed. And as it will commence during the sixth seal's timeframe and will include many different groups of people, one of the groups who will be terminated during this period will be the Jewish race.

Meanwhile, as this second round of genocide will lay claim to one third of the earth's populace that will include the Jewish race, according to Isaiah 62:2 the Lord's people who survived the first round of genocide will then be called by a new name. As this indicates the blessing of dawning radiance will make sufficient impression upon the earth's inhabitants that it will prompt a new name to refer to those who receive the blessing, assuming the blessing of dawning radiance will be something more than a simple visual type of photonic shining, the blessing of dawning radiance suggests it will be some form of enlightenment that will far surpass all intellectual reasoning seen today.

One possible example for how this may appear is the way some music shines considerably above and beyond those of lesser quality.

Besides the two descriptions of a blessing bestowed on day 1,335 and that of dawning radiance after a period of tribulation, another description to these events appears with Rev. 12:5–6 when describing the birth of a son to a woman who flees into the wilderness where God has prepared a retreat for her for twelve hundred sixty days.

As these 1,260 days transpire during the end of days period, the description of birth appears as another analogy in describing the dawning radiance in Isaiah 60:1 and 3, and the blessing on day 1,335 in Daniel 12:12.

And if these are the same, the retreat in the wilderness that God had prepared to care for the woman for 1,260 days would correlate with the transport of the Lord's people to the land of Israel that is described in Isaiah 49:22–23, 60:4, and 66:20 that will come after the tribulation period.

One issue this interpretation resolves is the misnomer many theologians have had that the 1,260–day depiction in Rev. 12:6 represented the tribulation period for the Lord's people but were at a loss to explain the one-month shortfall discrepancy with the tribulation depictions of forty-two months in Revelation 11:2 and 13:5 and 1,290 days in Daniel 12:11, all of which constitute a 3.5-year period as described in Daniel 12:7 and are one month longer than the 1,260-day period.

And with the 1,260-day retreat in the wilderness following the blessing on day 1,335 that will initiate the return of the Lord's people to the land of Israel, as Isaiah 60:2 describes, the world's inhabitants will be laying in darkness at the initiation of this event that will represent the fall of the beast's and antichrist's system, Daniel 7:11–12 further describe this period as when the beast (including the antichrist) will be slain and his body destroyed and handed over to be burned by fire, at which point the remaining three animals (socioeconomic systems) will be allowed to exist for a season and a time.

As the burning of the beast with fire correlates with various depictions of a global earthquake that will destroy all cities worldwide, at which time the world's cities will then lie vacant (Isaiah 6:11; Rev. 6:12; Rev. 16:18-9), with this indicating the commencement of another series of events following the days of tribulation in conjunction with the return of the Lord's people to the devastated land of Israel, these events will be more properly addressed in an upcoming volume so that events leading to this point may be more thoroughly addressed now.

When Rev. 12:11 portrays the Lord's people as those who "…have not loved their lives, even to the point of death," as this represents the tribulation period under the fourth and fifth seals' timeframes and is prior to the birth on day 1,335, it then describes the interim period between these two events.

Narrowing this timeframe further appears in the following verse. When Rev. 12:12 describes the devil's fall to earth (also depicted in Rev. 12:4 and 12:9, as the dragon with his angels being flung out and tossed to the ground), at which point the dragon then stations himself ready to devour the newborn on day 1335, this scripture then indicates the devil's shakeout from heaven (Hebrews 12:26–27) will occur at the end of the fifth seal's timeframe within the 45-day window from day 1,290 to 1,335.

As a result of being ousted from heaven, Rev. 12:12 then describes the dragon: "with raging anger, well aware that he has but a short season."

The following verses in Revelation 12:13–14 then relate how the dragon will initially direct his raging anger by pursuing the woman (God's spirit) who had given birth to the male child (the blessing of dawning radiance), but that she will be flown to her retreat in the wilderness (devastated Israel), where she will be exempt from any further tribulation for the next 1,260 days.

Despite having refuge in the devastated land of Israel, however, the dragon will continue his attempt to dispose of the woman, as the following verses in Revelation 12:15–17 relate:

> The serpent poured water like a river out of his mouth after
> the woman, that she might be swept away by the stream, but

the earth came to the woman's aid; the earth opened its mouth and swallowed the river which the dragon had poured from his mouth. And the dragon, enraged at the woman, went off to wage war against the rest of her offspring, who observe the commands of God and adhere to the testimony of Jesus. And he stood on the sandy seashore.

As the serpent (the devil) goes off to wage war against the rest of her offspring, the rest of her offspring represent the survivors of the tribulation who will then reside in the wilderness—the devastated land of Israel, exempt from further genocide for the next 1,260 days.

But, as Rev. 12:5 also describes her child snatched away up to God and His throne, these individuals represent all the Lord's people in Rev. 6:10 who appear in a state of limbo until their birth, at which time they are then described in Rev. 7:14–15 before God's throne, indicating the one and only rapture of God's people, prior to the Lord's return, of those who have gone through the great tribulation and have died as a result.

The waters the dragon will then pour out of his mouth like a river after the woman represent numerous points of reason his emissaries on earth will utilize to contest God's spirit and the lifestyle standards of the newborn survivors of the Lord's people residing in the devastated land of Israel. But as the earth will come to the woman's rescue, it indicates the serpent's contentious claims will not stand.

And as these claims are in conjunction with his standing on the sandy seashore (Rev. 12:17), it then specifies the means by which he will deceive the rest of the world's inhabitants until his claims collapse.

With the dragon standing on the sandy seashore in Rev. 12:17 and the following verse in Revelation 13:1 describing a beast with 10 horns and seven heads with 10 diadems (flags) on his horns emerging from the sea through authorization from the dragon in Rev. 13:2, it indicates that the beast will be granted the capacity to attain a source of energy from the sea that will be inexpensive and virtually unlimited.

But, as the earth will come to the woman's rescue by swallowing the waters poured out by the serpent, indicating the dragons assertions against God's Spirit will dissipate, it then indicates that the dragon's stance on the sandy seashore——inexpensive and abundant energy from the sea—will cause some type of severe environmental catastrophe.

This conjecture is further corroborated with Rev. 12:12 describing woe to both earth and sea as a result of the serpent being cast out of heaven, indicating the dragon will be fully aware of the ramifications involved in attaining the relatively inexpensive energy from the sea through the means he will provide the beast.

Another item this perspective clarifies is that while the data presented in Revelation 13:1–2 appear to describe a progression of events following those in Revelation chapter 12, with the description of the beast with 10 horns and seven heads emerging from the sea indicating a point in time prior to when the beast and antichrist are burned, Rev. 13:1–2 then represents a retrospective description to events described in Revelation chapter 12.

And with the following verse in Rev. 13:3 describing the fatally wounded head of the beast resuscitated, as this resuscitation will be the result of the abundant and inexpensive source of energy from the sea that at first will usher in global economic prosperity, with the world's inhabitants laying in darkness as described in Isaiah 60:2 when the blessing of dawning radiance is issued to the Lord's people on day 1,335, something will have caused the world's antichrists/atheists to have abandoned their hedonistic adoration for the dragon and the beast, thereby indicating an environmental collapse will have resulted from the source of energy the dragon will have provided the beast considerably prior to his having been ousted from heaven.

This, however, raises the issue that if the source of relatively abundant and inexpensive energy from the sea will become available to the beast considerably prior to birth on day 1,335 of the Lord's people, then how is it that the dragon once ousted from heaven will station himself just prior to this birth ready to devour the newborn? The answer to this is the presumption that when the dragon stands on the sandy seashore in Rev. 12:17 and bestows power and authority to the beast in Rev. 13:2, this represents a linear event in time after his having been ousted from heaven when he stations himself ready to devour the newborn on day 1,335.

But as the dragon will stand on the source of energy he will provide the beast that will usher in economic prosperity, to do so would indicate that this source of energy would have to already have been in place when he pours out rivers of contentious arguments against those of opposing views after their birth occurs on day 1,335.

In which case, Rev. 13:1–4 represents a retrospective description of events leading to birth on day 1,335. And as Rev. 13:4 describes the world worshiping the dragon and the beast resulting from the economic prosperity the source of energy from the sea will usher in, the word "worship" in this scripture describes an adoration the world will have towards the lifestyle derived from the mass quantity of goods that will be available; Revelation chapters 17 and 18 describe this adoration based on materialistic gratification, as sensuality, wantonness, and passionate immorality, which, according to Ephesians 4:19, describe the character of those who abandon themselves to sensuality as troubled by no compunctions, "…so as to practice with greediness all kinds of impurity."

And with greediness synonymous with idolatry (Ephesians 5:5 and Corinthians 3:5), which leads to faithlessness (1 Timothy 6:9–10), it then connotes those choosing to worship a materialistic lifestyle will gradually loose faith in God by replacing God in their lives with things (idols) as their god.

This perspective is substantiated with Isaiah 2:8–9 stating, "… they worship (love) the work of their own hands, that which their fingers have fashioned. Accordingly, man lowers himself, and even the more respectable man is brought down."

While some may see this scripture as relating to idols representing deities, as another reference from Luke 12:34 quotes: "For where your treasure is, there too your heart will be" it clearly indicates what one values is where ones love lies. And if one's affections are more materialistically inclined, where things (idols) have become what certain individuals' love, the less spiritually inclined towards God such individuals will be.

And as Revelation chapters 17 and 18 describe, most of mankind will worship a sensual lifestyle during the reign of the antichrist and the beast; immorality through idolatry through faithlessness then appears the reason why approximately 75 percent of mankind will become antichrists/atheists, having replaced faith in God with a love for idolatry, and thereby lowering their moral standards accordingly.

To contact author with a question: louisdiedricks@yahoo.com

BIBLIOGRAPHY

"The Arab World: Oil, Power, Violence." *Time Magazine* Vol.101 No 14, 1973. (accessed 6/25/2008)

"Birth of Christ." Wikipedia (2009). http://en.wikipedia.org/ Birth_of_Christ (accessed 3/9/2009)

Carney, Matthew. "The New Libya." *Dateline* (2003): [pages] http://news.sbs.com.au/dateline/the_new_libya_130300 accessed 5/15/2008

Diedricks, Louis. *What It Is, Vol.1: Geschichte.* Minneapolis: Mill City Press, 2008.

Kosmin, Barry A. and Ariela Keysar. "American Nones: The Profile of the No Religion Popultation."*American Religious Identification Survey* (2008). http://www.americanreligionsurvey-aris.org/ (accessed on 3/11/2009)

Manning, Jennifer. pg 67 Dust to Gust: 12-28-2006 http://www.eurealert.org/pub_releases/2006-12/acft-dtg122806.php (accessed on 12/18/2008)

"Monsters of the Past" *History Channel.*

"Number of the beast" Wikipedia (2009). http://en.wikipedia.org/Number_of_the_beast (accessed 3/2/2008)

Omestead, Thomas. "Libya Moves Back Into Circulation." *US News & World Report* (2007): [pgs. 31-32]

"Religions." Wikipedia (2009). http://en.wikipedia.org/wiki/Religions (accessed on 3/19/2009)

Tolme, Paul. "Get Ready to Itch & Sneeze." *Newsweek* (August 11, 2008) [pg. 52]

Walsh, Bryan. "CNN: ENVIRONMENT: Planet in Peril: Dying for A Drink." *Time Magazine* [Vol 172 No 24] (12/4/2008): [pages 46-49].